Unleashing the Power of Music

Sound Therapy for Well-Being

Table of Contents

Chapter 1. Introduction

Unleash a new wave of harmony within yourself with the power of music! Our special report, "Unleashing the Power of Music: Sound Therapy for Well-Being," provides a fresh look at the profound effect of sound on our emotional and physical health. With a spirit of joy and wisdom, it takes you on a melodious journey, exploring how the rhythmic entrainment of music influences our mood and consciousness, how melodies relieve stress and promote healing, and why the symphony of sound is the underappreciated medicine we all need. Woven with real-life stories, expert insights, and practical techniques, this report is not just about gaining knowledge - it's an immersive experience. So why wait? Tune in to this harmonious wonder, and open the door to resonant wellness that awaits your discovery within these pages!

Chapter 2. The Harmony of Health: An Overview

The sound of our heartbeat, the rhythm of our breath, the pulsating of our neurons - our bodies are deeply connected to the music of life. Given this inherent bond, it is no surprise that sound and music wield an impressive influence over our health and wellbeing.

2.1. The Rhythmic Alignment of Body and Mind

The intimate relationship between music and health begins in the womb. A fetus's first auditory experience is the steady rhythm of the mother's heartbeat, a prelude to its forthcoming journey filled with sound. Upon birth, our bond with rhythm only strengthens as it syncs with our biological processes - our heartbeats, blood flow, breathing patterns, sleep cycles, and daily routines.

This rhythmic entrainment acts as an orchestra conductor, coordinating the tempo of our body and mind. And just as a melody can change the mood of a scene in a film, the rhythms in our lives can influence our emotions, behaviors, and health.

Research corroborates this, showing rhythm's role in managing stress, enhancing motor abilities, and facilitating cognitive functioning. Rhythmic auditory stimulation, for instance, has assisted Parkinson's patients in improving their gait, and babies exposed to rhythmic patterns demonstrated better neural responses.

2.2. The Cadence of Consciousness

Music, in its varying forms, extends its influence to our consciousness. The entrainment of our brainwaves into the rhythm of a sound has been demonstrated through a process called frequency following response (FFR). This process enables our brainwaves to align with the frequency of an external sound.

Dozens of studies showcase how FFR can modulate our conscious states. Slow, repetitive energy drumming, for instance, can shift our consciousness from a regular wakeful state to a deeply meditative one. Conversely, quicker tempos can engender alertness and higher cognitive function.

Typically, our brain produces delta waves in deep sleep, theta waves in drowsiness and light sleep, alpha waves in relaxed awareness, beta waves when alert, and gamma waves during higher processing tasks. Music, acting as respective stimuli, can coax our brains into these states, influencing our creativity, focus, relaxation, learning, and more.

2.3. Melodies of Medicine

The therapeutic potential of music has long been recognized by various cultures, and modern medicine has followed suit. Therapeutic techniques that harness the power of music, such as music therapy and sound therapy, have become integral in contemporary medical practices. Even the World Health Organization underlines the importance of such arts-bound interventions for health and well-being.

In a clinical setting, music has been shown to alleviate pain, reduce the side effects of chemotherapy, assist in physical rehab and stroke recovery, and manage symptoms of mental health disorders like depression and anxiety.

Music therapy's modus operandi often relies on the creation of personalized 'soundscapes' - unique sound environments that resonate with the individual's needs and preferences, providing calming and healing experiences. It's not merely passive listening;

engagement with music - such as singing, tapping, and composing - sparks creativity and provides powerful catharsis.

2.4. Resounding Resilience

Moreover, engaging with music can help cultivate resilience. The process of making music can foster empowerment, agency, and hope - especially valuable during times of intense stress or trauma. Musical engagement stimulates a broad range of neurochemical responses that can offset adverse physical and psychological reactions associated with stress.

Comforting hormones like oxytocin, often released during moments of musical engagement, counteract the effects of stress hormones like cortisol. Hence, using music as a medium of self-expression can shift one's emotional state, building resilience and emotional intelligence over time.

2.5. The Understated Instruments of Inner Harmony

The world of musical instruments is diverse and far-reaching. Traditional instruments like the Tibetan singing bowls or the Aboriginal didgeridoo, alongside modern innovations like biofeedback instruments, have surfaced in the wellness sphere.

These acoustic remedies offer relief both through their inherent musical properties and the act of playing them. Rhythmic drumming, for instance, synchronizes the left and right brain hemispheres, encouraging emotional release and reducing anxiety. Even the vibrations from a tuning fork can evoke relaxation by activating specific energy centers or 'chakras'.

In conclusion, humanity's bond with music is indissoluble. The rhythm that pulses through us is inextricably linked to the rhythm that beats around us. Recognizing the healing potential of sound and music can transform the orchestra of our lives, ameliorating not merely our physical health but the harmony of our very being too. The melody of well-being is awaiting its composition. Listen closely, for it is within you, ready to create a symphony of health and happiness.

Chapter 3. Music and Emotion: Interweaving Melodies and Feelings

The bond between music and emotion is an ancient one, reaching back into the mists of pre-history and beyond. Today, we continue to explore the enduring relationship between melody and feeling, unraveling the layered complexities that imbue our lives with resonance and meaning, chord by chord, note by note.

3.1. The Physiology of Feeling

Emotions are a complicated physiological phenomena, but one that is intimately related to the music we hear. When we listen to a piece of music, our brain processes the sound waves, converting them into electrical signals that are sent to various regions. When these signals reach the amygdala, a part of the brain involved in emotion regulation, a series of chemical reactions is triggered.

In response to the brain's processing of music, the body may release certain hormones and neurotransmitters, such as dopamine and serotonin, which are associated with feelings of pleasure and happiness. At the same time, listening to music may also attenuate the production of cortisol, the body's main stress hormone. This explains why music often soothes us during stressful times.

Music can also evoke intense feelings of nostalgia, a response initiated by the hippocampus, an area of the brain fundamental for memory formation. When we associate a song with a specific memory or event, hearing that song can transport us back to that moment, vividly re-experiencing emotions of those times.

3.2. A Symphony of Sentiments

Music's power to elicit a broad range of emotions is a testament to its versatility and expressive depth. Scholars broadly categorize the emotions elicited by music into three categories: perceived emotions, felt emotions, and blended emotions.

Perceived emotions are those that are recognized in the music but not necessarily felt by the listener. You may perceive sadness in a piece of music without feeling sad yourself. Conversely, felt emotions refer to the feelings that are incited in you when you hear a piece of music. When a song makes you feel happy, that's a felt emotion.

Blended emotions occur when you feel an emotion that's different from those perceived in the music. For instance, a somber melody might inspire feelings of tranquility rather than the anticipated sadness. This intriguing occurrence underpins the multifaceted relationship between sound and sentiment, opening avenues for therapeutic applications.

3.3. Resonating with Emotion: The Role of Musical Elements

Different musical elements can evoke various emotions. The tempo or speed of the rhythm can shift our mood. Fast-tempo music is often associated with happiness or excitement, while slow-tempo music can induce feelings of melancholy or relaxation.

Melody, the succession of musical notes, has a significant role in steering our emotional response. A sequence of rising pitches often expresses a sense of happiness or anticipation. Falling pitches, in contrast, can convey a melancholic or soothing feeling.

Harmony, the simultaneous combination of notes, is also crucial in the emotional response to music. Consonant harmonies—those with notes that sound complete or stable together—generally spark feelings of cheerfulness or calmness. Dissonant harmonies—those that seem incomplete or unstable—can stir feelings of tension, unease, or excitement, depending on the context.

Lastly, volume or dynamics plays its part too. A sudden switch from soft to loud can cause surprise or excitement, while a smooth decrescendo may soothe or sadden us.

3.4. Music Preferences and Personality

The type of music we gravitate towards often aligns with our personality traits, reflecting and reinforcing our emotional states. For instance, extraverted individuals tend to prefer upbeat, energetic genres, while those with a philosophical or complex personality might lean towards introspective or sophisticated styles of music.

Understanding the connection between our musical preferences and our emotions can offer valuable insights into our emotional well-being and aid in the development of music-based therapies.

3.5. The Role of Culture and Experience

Music and emotion are intrinsically linked to our cultural contexts and personal experiences. The emotional response to a certain type of music can drastically vary from individual to individual, and from culture to culture.

In Western societies, for example, major key music is often associated with joyous emotions while minor key music is associated with sadness. Yet in other cultures, this association may not stand. Our personal and cultural associations with specific musical characteristics guide our emotional responses to music.

Further, our individual experiences also play an essential role. If a particular song was playing during a distressing or jubilant event in our life, we might feel corresponding sadness or joy whenever we hear that song, even if the song in general wouldn't elicit such intense emotions.

3.6. Music Therapy: A Sound Practice

Psychologists and therapists have begun to harness the potent relationship between music and emotions to promote healing and well-being. Music therapy can be a powerful tool to assist in regulating emotions, alleviating anxiety and depression, and improving overall mental health.

Through guiding patients in creating, playing, or just listening to music, therapists can tap into a non-verbal, emotional communication channel. This allows individuals to express feelings that they might struggle to convey through words, creating a bridge to understanding, relief, and emotional growth.

Music's power to interweave melodies and feelings offers a unique journey into our emotional selves. As we continue to delve into this intricate relationship, we open the door to further understanding our emotional well-being and more profound methods of healing and self-discovery. Sound, as beautiful as it is therapeutic, is a phenomenon that resonates within each one of us, affecting our emotions and well-being in ways we are only beginning to comprehend. This harmonic dialogue, this symphony of sentiment, is our shared human anthem that rings true across cultures, ages, and individual hearts.

Chapter 4. From Rhythm to Relaxation: Stress Relief through Music

In a world that appears to move at breakneck speed, stress seems to have become an unwelcome companion for many. The burden of stress can lead to an array of health problems - both physical and mental. However, there is a surprisingly melodious solution to this problem: music. This chapter embarks on a journey, guiding you from the rhythm to relaxation, illuminating how music can be a proven, potent therapy for stress relief.

4.1. The Science of Stress

Stress, a biological response designed to protect us from threats, is not inherently harmful. Short-term or 'acute' stress can give you a boost of adrenaline and focus. However, problems arise when stress becomes a chronic condition. Chronic stress has been linked to a range of health issues, from depression and anxiety to heart disease and diabetes.

When we perceive danger, our bodies enter the 'fight or flight' mode. In this state, our bodies release adrenaline and cortisol, preparing us for imminent action. These chemicals increase heart rate, blood pressure, and glucose levels, offering energy boosts necessary for survival.

However, our bodies may not always differentiate between a harmful event and a stressful work situation. As a result, those enduring chronic stress remain in an almost constant 'fight or flight' mode, resulting in an overabundance of stress-related hormones. Over time, this situation can lead to significant health issues.

4.2. Music: A Natural Stress Reliever

At this juncture, understanding what we can do to relieve chronic stress is paramount. Enter Music! Our bodies' response to stress is an automatic one. However, music has a unique capacity to reach us on a subconscious level. Music, in its essence, is rhythm, and our bodies, amazingly, inherently respond to these rhythms.

Our hearts somehow synchronize with the rhythm and tempo of music. This entrainment allows slower-tempo music to induce relaxation by literally slowing our heart rates. A 2009 study in the journal Circulation showed that music, especially classical, could lower heart rates, blood pressure, and levels of cortisol. Furthermore, music has been shown to promote the release of endorphins, our bodies' natural 'feel-good' chemicals.

Combining these effects, music therapy can encourage biological changes that reduce stress and promote relaxation, a concept that has been guiding music therapists for years.

4.3. Practical Techniques for Stress Relief

Embarking on your musical stress relief requires a few essential techniques:

1. Active Listening: This is more than just letting music play in the background whilst completing other tasks. Active listening requires full attention; focus on the way the sounds and notes interplay, the emotions the music evokes. This mindful engagement can interrupt unnecessary stress thoughts.

2. Creating a Relaxing Music Playlist: The key here is personal preference. It's essential to explore and find what brings you tranquility. Scientifically, music with a slow tempo, low pitch, and

no lyrics has been found to be most beneficial for relaxation.

3. Singing/Shouting: Expressing emotions vocally can be therapeutic and release stress. Singing along to a favorite upbeat song or even shouting out the lyrics from a piece of heavy rock can be a great vent for pent-up feelings.

4. Playing an Instrument: Making music actively engages the brain, encouraging a focus on the positive, calming elements of reality. It requires concentration that can help drown out stressful thoughts. Plus, a study in the British Journal Annuals of the New York Academy of Sciences highlighted muscular relaxation, particularly in the upper body, when playing an instrument.

4.4. Music Therapy: Proven Alternative Medicine

Music therapy, a recognized health profession, is an established method used within health care systems for various applications. Therapists use music to forge a bond with patients, employing it as a vehicle to help process emotions. In the field of stress relief, therapists use techniques such as guided imagery (a process that includes creating peaceful images in the mind) in conjunction with music to release stress.

According to studies, music therapy has been successful in reducing anxiety before surgery, managing chronic pain, improving mood, and aiding relaxation in patients receiving chemotherapy treatment.

4.5. Conclusion

In the epic symphony of life, we often find ourselves facing the discordant notes of stress. However, the soothing strains of music serve as a compelling antidote that can help us regain harmony and equilibrium. As this chapter has shown, placing a well-curated playlist or a trusted musical instrument at the heart of your stress management plan can invite relaxation, peace, and well-being back into your life. Tune into the rhythm of relaxation and reclaim your inner tranquility today.

Chapter 5. The Beat of Your Heart: Rhythm and Physical Wellbeing

Music and rhythm have an encapsulating journey, deep-rooted in the synchronicity of life. You may wonder how it relates to your wellbeing or how it can make a difference in your biological resistance. To elaborate, let's delve deeper into the nuances of rhythm and its connective resonance with our physical wellbeing.

5.1. The Pulse of Life: Rhythm Embedded Within Us

Our natural world pulsates with rhythm. Each wave that crashes against the shore, each bird that sings at the break of dawn, every flower that unfurls to greet the morning sun, they all hold a unique rhythm, which reinstates the inevitable presence of rhythm in our universe. But perhaps the most intricate and intimate rhythm lies within us: our heartbeat.

The human heart is a rhythmic powerhouse. With an average rate of 60 to 100 beats per minute, the heart sets an incessant tempo, circulating blood and nutrients to every corner of our body, mirroring our emotional states, moods, and overall health. This rhythm automatically adjusts to our body's demands; it elevates when we exercise, it drops as we rest - an unplanned symphony conducted through life itself.

5.2. Echoes of the Heart: How Music Mimics our Rhythm

Music, in every culture, remains intrinsically bound with rhythm. It is an auditory reflection, a sonic portrayal of our internal cadence. Natural rhythms found in music echo the rhythms found in our bodies, specifically our heartbeats.

When you listen to a piece of music, your body instinctively seeks to align with the rhythm. This instinctive phenomenon, known as "entrainment," allows the human heartbeat to synchronize with the metronomic beat of music. From tribal drumming circles to pulsating techno music, the power of rhythm in music to entrain our heart rate is profoundly universal.

Consequently, tempo and genre of the music we listen to could significantly impact how we feel physically. Upbeat music with a high tempo can make us feel animated and energetic, while slower, more melodic music can help us relax.

5.3. A Harmonious Health Booster: Music's Impact on Our Physical Health

Music's capacity to affect our heart rate and other bodily functions has led to robust connections between music, sound therapy, and health outcomes. For instance, research has shown that listening to calming music can lower blood pressure, steady the heart rate, and reduce stress-related hormones, cumulatively impacting our wellbeing positively.

1. Lowering stress: Stress is the antithesis of wellbeing and can cause several physical issues ranging from heart problems to

immunity disorders. The soothing properties of music, especially pieces with a slower tempo, stimulate our parasympathetic system, helping our bodies return to a calm and relaxed state.

2. Pain management: Several studies suggest music can help alleviate pain. Its rhythmic aspect, combined with melodic and harmonic structures, can draw an individual's attention away from the pain, creating a form of auditory analgesia.

3. Boosting immunity: Positive emotions aroused by music influence our immune system. The joy, excitement, or relaxation we often feel can trigger biochemical changes that boost our immunity, further contributing to our health.

5.4. The Healing Symphony: Tailoring Your Personal Sonic Therapy

Listening to the harmonic chords and rhythmic beats can indeed bring splendid improvements in your health. It's a matter of identifying what works best for you. Here is a guide on how to form a therapeutic relationship with music:

1. Listen attentively: Active engagement is crucial for music therapy. Focused listening allows us to fully experience the rhythmic alignment, thus enhancing our cognitive and emotional responses.

2. Embrace variety: Music is as diverse as people in the world. Delve into various genres, moods and find the rhythms that truly speak to you.

3. Let it resonate: Music isn't just an auditory experience. Allow your body to feel the pulsating beats, vibrating strings, and rhythmic melodies.

4. Create your playlist: Make a collection of tracks that have a

beneficial influence on your wellbeing. Keep it updated and handy for your daily routine.

5. Reflect on your feelings: Music harnesses the power of introspection. Use these musical moments to navigate and understand your emotional state better.

5.5. Toward a Song-Filled Tomorrow

Indeed, rhythm in music has far-reaching impacts on our physical health and wellbeing. As we begin to understand the profound connections, it offers a potential window into unexplored healing. It reminds us of our ancestral connection to rhythm and music.

The symphony of life continues with each beat of your heart. Music is not outside us but within us, resonating with our life's rhythm, an unseen force propelling our wellbeing. By tuning into this melodious journey, we can unleash a new wave of harmony within ourselves, heralding a song-filled tomorrow.

Chapter 6. Voices of Nature: Sonic Therapy Beyond Music

From the subtle murmur of a gentle brook to the melodious tunes of chirping birds, the sounds of nature have been a source of solace and rejuvenation for humans since time immemorial. Across the globe, amidst the hustle and bustle of urban life, individuals seek refuge in natural surroundings to soak in the tranquility that is often lacking in their everyday environments.

6.1. The Healing Properties of Nature's Sounds

Numerous scientific studies have endorsed the restorative power of natural sounds. From improving mood to reducing stress, promoting sleep, cognitive performance, and more – these studies illuminate why our penchant for nature is beyond an aesthetic attraction.

In Japan, a practice known as 'Shinrin-yoku,' or 'forest bathing,' has been recognized as a form of nature therapy since the 1980s. It involves immersing oneself in the forest atmosphere and soaking in its sounds. Research on Shinrin-yoku participants showed improved mood, reduced stress levels, and enhanced immune system functioning, among other benefits.

A study by Rachel Kaplan at the University of Michigan delved into the effects of nature on cognitive fatigue. The participants who were exposed to natural sounds had significantly better performance on cognitively demanding tasks than those exposed to urban sounds, illustrating how nature's symphony could boost cognitive abilities.

6.2. Soundscapes and Walking Meditation

In addition to being a balm for stressed minds, nature's sounds lend themselves powerfully to another ancient practice – walking meditation. Practitioners of the mindfulness-based approach focus their senses as they walk slowly, taking deep, measured breaths in sync with their steps and attuning their ears to nature's immaculate soundscapes. This gentle rhythm promotes a more profound sense of self-awareness, inherently calming the mind.

The Californian firm, Field, specializes in creating software for natural soundscape synthesis. They provide an immersive auditory environment for their users, increasing their focus and creating a sense of serenity amidst their busy lives, demonstrating how technology can serve as a bridge, bringing nature's solace to urbanites.

6.3. Echoes of the Past: Ancestral Soundscape Appreciation

Human appreciation of nature's sounds isn't just a contemporary phenomenon but likely a deeply ingrained evolutionary trait. Ancestral humans relied heavily on sounds for survival; a rustle in the leaves might indicate an approaching predator, while a stream's babble would signify a source of freshwater.

Anthropologists speculate that our strong emotional responses to nature's sounds today may be remnants of these ancestral cues, implying that our affinity for the sonic aspects of the natural world is deeply woven into our biological fabric.

The fields' soothing rustle, streams' bubbling gurgle, or a bird's cheerful chirp can do more than merely delight our ears. These sounds hold promising therapeutic potential. They can anchor us in the present, alleviate our cognitive fatigue, and provide us with a nurturing framework for meditation.

6.4. Biomusic: The Rhythm of Life

Biomusic is another subfield where the rhythms and patterns in biological phenomena inspire music. From melodies mimicking bird songs to rhythms calibrated according to the heartbeat, biomusic presents an innovative and potentially healing dimension of tuning in with nature.

Life's processes have a rhythm and meter of their own: consider the regular pulse of heartbeats or the cyclic crescendo and decrescendo of breathing. Musicians and therapists strive to harness these natural patterns. They attempt to attune individuals to their innate rhythmic sense, promoting synchronization within the body.

6.5. Final Thought: Nature's Sonic Symphony

Paying attention to the vibrant orchestra of nature promises a surprisingly rich sonic experience. Whether offering the restorative calm of a forest stream or the heartbeat's rhythmic reassurances, these sounds awaken a profound sense of harmony and contentment within us. Exploring this fascinating realm of sound therapy takes us one step further in understanding how listening can enhance well-being and emotional equilibrium.

Counterbalancing the cacophony of our modern existence with nature's serenade is crucial. Recognizing the pervasive influence of sonic environments on our well-being, we stand poised on the threshold of a new appreciation for the role of sound in achieving a healthier, more balanced life. From quiet introspection amidst bird songs to the deep tranquility inspired by forest sounds - sonic nature therapy is an underexplored but potent aspect of holistic self-care. As we move forward, let's strive to tune into nature's symphony and weave these nuanced acoustic threads into the fabric our daily lives, awaiting the lasting resonance of their healing touch.

Chapter 7. Humming, Chants, and Mantras: Traditional Approaches to Sound Therapy

Sound therapy is indeed an ancient practice that permeates various cultures and traditions worldwide. From the hums of the Tibetan monks to the resonating melodies of the Gregorian chants, the therapeutic value of vocal sounds has a long and rich history.

7.1. Humbly Humming

People often hum to themselves, perhaps unknowingly as a source of comfort or to induce a peaceful state. Scientifically, humming has been found to invoke relaxation by activating the part of the brain that triggers calmness and tranquility.

Through the act of humming, our bodies are filled with vibrations that resound from our heads to our toes. These vibrations, in turn, stimulate the circulatory system and allow for increased oxygenation of the body. Furthermore, humming can create a massaging effect within our bodies leading to improved function of our internal organs.

Moreover, the pattern and resonance of humming play a vital role in the effect it can have on one's mind and body. The steady, slow rhythm of a hum can help slow our heart rate, steady our breathing, and relax our muscles, thereby improving our mental health indirectly.

7.2. Mantras and Chants: The Voices of Tranquility

The use of mantras and chants, deeply rooted in traditions, serve as another significant form of sound therapy. These spiritual or religious vocal sequences communicate profound psychological and physical healing effects.

Mantras, short phrases or words, often devoid of inherent meaning, are repetitively chanted to create a meditative state. On the other hand, chants are usually longer and may carry specific meanings, each intended to evoke specific emotional and spiritual states.

The ancient Vedic civilizations of India propagated the use of Sanskrit mantras to achieve higher consciousness. Chants with complex musical arrangements transcended common understanding and were used to usher participants into transcendent states.

Positive changes at the cellular level have been demonstrated in scientific studies with mantra chanting. Chanting aids in slowing down brain waves, inducing a state of deep relaxation, often akin to the beneficial effects of sleep. These processes help reduce anxiety and promote a general sense of well-being.

Repetitive chanting or mantra recitation can create a sort of sound current. This sonic current captivates the mind, drawing away from other distractions. It is similar to the flow state achieved in deep work or creative activities.

This ability to observe rather than participate in the thought process is a fundamental aspect of mindfulness, a constituent of mental well-being and stress reduction that can empower individuals to take control of their own mental health.

7.3. Traditional Applications: Healing to Enlightenment

Across global traditions, this understanding and application of sound therapy manifest in various ways. Indigenous cultures sought spiritual healing and connection with the universe through the rhythms of deliberate speech and song.

Whether it's the reverberating drone of the didgeridoo in ritualistic healing practices of the Australian aborigines, the spiritual Native American medicine songs, or the rhythmic recitation of the Quran in Islam, sound therapy's restorative power transcends barriers of geography and time.

Shamanic journeys often involve characteristic drumming patterns, guiding participants into non-ordinary states of consciousness for healing and spiritual insights. In Buddhism, specific sound patterns or 'dharanis' are recited to remove hindrances and unlock enlightened wisdom.

In essence, these traditional sound therapy strategies are keys to accessing deeper levels of consciousness, connecting with the self and the divine, promoting health and balance, and constructing a meaningful, holistic wellbeing.

7.4. Going Forward: Harnessing the Power

Acknowledging and harnessing the healing qualities of hums, chants, and mantras can be a life-changing adventure. By regularly practicing humming or chanting, one can significantly help the mind slow down, overcome stress, and promote relaxation and positivity. These practices can be a pathway to stronger emotional resilience, improved focus, and general cognitive well-being.

Like a well-composed symphony brings peace to a chaotic mind, regulating our breath with the rhythm of the hums and orienting our mental presence with the chants and mantras can help us tune into wellness. Let us indeed swing to the symphony of sounds, for it is a melodious journey towards attunement, harmony, and tranquility.

After all, it is not all about the destination; equally important is to enjoy the process, to live each hum, each mantra, each chant, navigate our emotional ebb, and flow with grace and fluidity.

This chapter provides a foundational understanding of the potential of humming, chanting, and mantra recitation, which are only a few of the numerous therapeutic sound techniques rooted in global traditions. As you unfold further pieces of this sound therapy tapestry, you will uncover more powerful yet subtler techniques, each promising a unique, harmonious journey encapsulating profound means of healing and transformation.

Chapter 8. Sound Meditation and Brainwaves: An Inside Story

As we delve deeper into the relationship between sound, meditation, and brainwaves, it's essential to lay a solid foundation of understanding. We will start with the elemental building block of all sound - vibration.

8.1. Understanding Vibration

Vibration, also known as oscillation, is a fundamental principle of the universe. It governs everything from the subatomic pulses at the heart of atoms to the rhythmic cycling of galaxies.

Sound, as we perceive it, is a type of vibration. Each note or tone carries a specific frequency or set of frequencies, each of which stimulates our ears (and, in turn, our brains) in a unique way. These vibratory inputs don't merely passively traverse our auditory system; they actively influence our states of consciousness, from the physical and emotional to the mental and spiritual.

8.2. The Physics of Sound

If we understand sound in the context of physics, it becomes clearer how it can induce profound impacts on our well-being. Physicists describe sound as longitudinal waves that move through a medium - such as air, water, or solid matter. These waves get picked up by our eardrums, and our brain translates them into what we perceive as sound.

The principle of 'resonance' is especially relevant. When one object vibrating at the same natural frequency as a second object forces that second object into vibrational motion, it's called resonance. When specific harmonious sounds resonate with corresponding brainwave patterns, they can stimulate distinct states of consciousness.

8.3. Your Brain on Different Frequencies

The human brain operates at various frequencies, each correlating with different states of consciousness. Delta (0.5-4 Hz) is the frequency of deep, dreamless sleep. Theta (4-8 Hz) signifies deep relaxation and meditation. Alpha (8-12 Hz) corresponds to relaxed states of alertness and creativity. Beta (12-30 Hz) represents normal waking consciousness, full of active thought. Finally, Gamma (30-100 Hz) is associated with high-level information processing and insight.

8.4. The Science of Entrainment

The notion of 'entrainment' is central here. First discovered in the 17th century by Dutch scientist Christiaan Huygens, entrainment is the process by which two rhythmic beings gradually synchronize to each other's rhythm. Chiming in with the state of human consciousness and brainwave frequencies, sound (especially rhythmical sound or music) can guide the brain into resonance with its frequency. This neural synchronization is what we mean by 'brainwave entrainment.'

8.5. Sound Meditation: A Path To Altered States of Consciousness

Sound meditation employs the principle of entrainment, using sounds with particular frequencies to guide your brainwaves into a desired state. A meditator might use a drum beat at the theta frequency to induce a deep meditative state, or a recording of ocean waves at the alpha frequency to encourage relaxation.

Using brainwave entrainment through sound meditation, you can consciously control your biological tuning. Tuning your brainwave frequencies to align with your desired state of consciousness can facilitate a variety of health and welfare benefits, such as stress reduction, pain relief, improvement in cognitive functions, better sleep, and enhanced creative abilities.

8.6. Techniques of Sound Meditation

Not all sound meditation involves sophisticated audio technology or musical instruments. Some of the most straightforward techniques use your body's natural resonators - your voice, your hands, your breath.

- Vocal toning: This technique involves making a prolonged, drone-like sound, typically on a single vowel. The process can trigger robust vibrational sensations throughout the body and help attune your consciousness to a calm and focused state.

- Body percussion: Rhythmical tapping or patting your body, particularly the chest, can not only create a range of interesting sounds but can also stimulate physical relaxation and emotional release.

- Breathing rhythms: Conscious manipulation of the breath, as seen in practices like pranayama in yoga, doesn't produce audible sound but employs a similar rhythmical entrainment principle.

8.7. In Conclusion

Whether you call it sound meditation, sound therapy, or brainwave entrainment, the practice of shaping consciousness through rhythm and tones has vast potential benefits. It can serve as a profound tool for self-care and healing, not to mention an exciting frontier for scientific research.

Remember that, like any other practice, sound meditation requires time, patience, and consistency. Experiment with different techniques, be open to the experiences they bring, and allow your consciousness to flow with the harmonious vibrations of the universe. The fascinating interplay of sound, meditation, and brainwaves is an incredible journey of self-discovery and well-being, waiting for you to embark upon. Don't miss the melody.

Chapter 9. Amplifying Healing: Clinical Cases of Music and Sound Therapy

Throughout time, music and sound therapy has been used to foster health and well-being. Recent research has brought to light how these therapies can help with a range of disorders, from depression to cancer, showing that we are only beginning to understand the vast potential they hold.

9.1. The Science of Sound

Let's begin by journeying into the fundamental principles that govern sound as a therapeutic construct. Be it the booming resonance of a bass guitar or the gentle whisper of a violin, sounds exist as unique sonic signatures or frequencies. The human body, too, operates on specific frequencies, each organ or body part vibrating at its distinct frequency.

Hence, when our body is exposed to external sound frequencies, especially ones that share harmonic relationships with our internal frequencies, a phenomenon known as 'resonance' takes place. This is analogous to pushing a swing at its natural frequency. The more we push it in harmony with its frequency, the higher it goes. This is the core concept behind sound therapy – aligning and harmonizing our internal vibrations with the help of external sound frequencies.

9.2. Impact of Sound Therapy: A Deep Dive

To understand the actual impact and scale, we penned down some real-life portrayals from various clinical case studies involving sound and music therapy.

Sharon is a 55-year-old woman battling breast cancer. She began undergoing chemotherapy and was reeling with the side effects – nausea, fatigue, and a tangible loss of hope. Her oncologist suggested integrating music therapy into her healing regime. Starting with simple musical exercises and gradually moving on to personalized playlists, tailored to sync with her body and mind at different phases of treatment. After a few weeks, Sharon reported feeling significantly calm and energized, despite the rigorous chemotherapy sessions.

Just as Sharon's is a case of using music to manage physical health issues, music therapy also holds vast potential in the realm of mental health.

Consider the case of Alex, a 40-year-old man diagnosed with clinical depression and anxiety. His mental health made him prone to intense mood swings and hampered his capacity to lead a balanced life. With directed sound therapy, involving binaural beats to alter brainwave patterns, Alex began to experience a decrease in anxiety levels, improvement in sleep patterns, and a general uplifting of moods. His journey underscores the profound potential that sound therapy holds for mental well-being.

9.3. Different Techniques, Different Effects

Each sound therapy technique could be deployed in a myriad of ways. Take the case of Vibroacoustic therapy (VAT), where low-frequency sound is transmitted into the body through specially designed speakers embedded in a recliner.

In a study, it was observed that patients with fibromyalgia who received VAT treatment for five weeks showed significant improvement. There was a decrease in pain intensity, enhanced quality of sleep, and increased overall quality of life indicating the immense potential VAT holds in improving physical health.

On the mental health front, studies have shown the benefits of techniques like chanting and humming. In a study on patients with severe Alzheimer's, regular sessions of chanting significantly improved mood and cognition levels.

9.4. Case of Group Music Therapy

Group music therapy often benefits those suffering from conditions like Post-Traumatic Stress Disorder (PTSD). People like Laura, a 30-year-old war veteran struggling with PTSD, underwent group music therapy where they created and played music as a form of expression. This method not only helped her express unresolved feelings, but the process also encouraged a deeper connection with others in her group, facilitating her journey towards healing.

9.5. Conclusion: The Road Ahead

In summary, a significant number of case studies have shown the potent healing effects of sound therapy. While more extensive research is warranted, it's clear that the application of sound and music therapies can aid in overcoming both physical and mental health struggles.

The journey through these clinical cases is echoic of the truth that therapeutic sound isn't merely about the hearing but more about the experience, which resonates within every cell, bringing about a harmonious wellness that can transform lives. Indeed, in the orchestra of life, tuning into the right frequency could be the melody that amplifies healing.

Chapter 10. Tuning into Your Inner Self: Practical Techniques for Musical Wellbeing

Sound as a pathway to inner peace has long been valued in ancient traditions. Music, as an integral part of human experience, has specific properties that can promote physical and emotional healing. This section will delve deep into these properties and present specific techniques for leveraging the power of music for improved wellbeing.

10.1. Tuning in with the Body

To understand the profound effect of music properly, we need to begin with the physical response it engenders. Music elicits a direct and immediate response not just in our ears, but in our hearts, brains, and throughout the body.

Scientific research supports these observations with data. According to neuroscientists, our brains and bodies react to rhythms, melodies, and harmonies in remarkable ways. Active and passive engagement with music can stimulate the brain, influence our heart rates, lower blood pressure, reduce stress, and even improve motor skills.

Practical techniques to help us use music for physical healing and wellbeing include:

1. Listening to slow tempo music, such as classical or lounge, to slow down heart rate and relax the body.
2. Engaging in active music making, such as drumming or singing, to boost motor skills.

3. Using upbeat music during exercise to maintain motivation and endurance.

10.2. Being Present

Music's impact extends beyond just the physical. It also helps us to attune ourselves to the present moment, a critical aspect of achieving mental well-being.

Mindful listening is a powerful practice that combines the therapeutic properties of music with the concentrating benefits of mindfulness. Like meditation, mindful listening asks us to focus our complete attention to the activity at hand: listening to music.

This practice starts with the selection of a particular piece of music that you find calming or uplifting. Next, enjoy the music and actively focus your attention on the melody, the harmony, the tempo, the way each note feeds into another, the silence between the notes - absorb every single detail.

Here are the steps to practice mindful listening:

1. Select a piece of music you enjoy.

2. Find a quiet environment where you won't be disturbed.

3. Close your eyes and focus solely on the music. Ignore all other thoughts.

4. Pay attention to every detail: the instruments, the melody, the vocals, the rhythm, etc.

5. End this practice with a few moments of silence, letting the sounds resonate within you.

10.3. Harmonizing Emotions with Music

Humans are emotional beings, and music is a powerful emotional stimulant.

Music can evoke a wide range of emotions - from joy to sorrow, excitement to tranquility. Knowing this, we can use music as a tool for emotional well-being.

Listeners can use certain songs or compositions to mirror their emotional state, which can lead to emotional validation. Alternatively, music can create an emotional counterpoint, providing an uplifting backdrop against feelings of sadness, or a calming influence in moments of high energy or stress.

Here's a way to use music for emotional healing:

1. Identify your current emotional state.

2. Choose a piece of music that either matches or counteracts this emotional state.

3. As you listen, let yourself fully embrace the emotion.

10.4. Music as a Bridge to Higher Consciousness

In many cultures, music, particularly rhythmic music like drumming or chanting, serves as a vehicle for achieving altered states of consciousness. This happens because of the ability of rhythmic sounds to affect brainwave activity.

Music doesn't have to be complex or orchestrated to have these effects. Simple drum beats, ambient music, or natural sounds, like the ocean's waves, can all induce brainwave entrainment, a state where brainwave frequency aligns with the rhythm of auditory stimuli. This, in turn, facilitates states of deep relaxation, meditative trance, or enhanced focus.

To use music for shifting consciousness, follow these steps:

1. Choose a piece of rhythmic music or a soundscape that you find soothing.

2. Find a quiet and comfortable location.

3. Close your eyes and concentrate wholly on the sound.

4. Let the music guide your internal rhythm.

10.5. In Conclusion

The practical techniques shared in this section provide a doorway into harnessing the inherent healing power of music. The journey starts with gaining an understanding of the effects of music on our physical being, our emotions, and our consciousness. As we learn to tune into our inner selves via the medium of music, it's important to remember that our experience will be personal and subjective, and that the most important thing is to approach the practice with openness and curiosity. May your journey through the melodies and harmonies not only bring sound into your ears but resonate wellness in your heart!

Chapter 11. Creating Your Sound Sanctuary: A Personalized Guide

Creating your sound sanctuary is an individual yet integrative process. It's like painting on the canvas of stillness with sounds as vibrant colors gracing the ears. The crux of creating a sound sanctuary lies in understanding, experimenting, and finally nurturing harmony in your personal spaces. This guide aims to facilitate the essence and exploration of sound, helping you design a space that nourishes wellness, serenity, and self-connection.

11.1. Understanding Your Sound Sanctuary

The first step towards sculpting your sound sanctuary is to comprehend what it means. A sound sanctuary is a personalized space—physical or imaginary, where the power of sound and silence intertwine to curate a serene, healing atmosphere. It's not just about creating a space filled with music. It's about mindfully selecting and infusing sounds that resonate with your spirit and evoke a sense of inner peace.

Just as each of us has a unique fingerprint, our resonance with certain sounds differs too. Some may find solace in the gentle tinkle of wind chimes, while for others, it could be the profound vibration of a Tibetan singing bowl that calms the mind.

11.2. The Role of Music Preferences

Every individual resonates differently with various genres of music.

Classical music might ignite peace within one person, while another might resonate more with the vigor of rock or the abstract tranquil beats of ambient music. Hence, identifying your personal preference plays a significant role.

You could explore different genres, artists, and compositions to figure out what resonates best with your emotions. For instance, you might detect a residual sweetness within your mind when engaging with mellifluous acoustic guitar pieces, or feel a wave of serenity pulsing through you when soaking in soothing instrumental music.

11.3. Tones, Frequencies, and their Impacts

In the landscape of sound therapy, individual tones and frequencies play significant roles in shaping our physiological responses. Certain frequencies are said to have specific effects, such as 432 Hz, often referred to as the "natural frequency of the Universe", which purportedly connects with the heart chakra and promotes emotional healing.

Similarly, binaural beats—a form of soundwave therapy, are created when two slightly different frequencies are presented separately to the left and right ears. The brain perceives a single new frequency from the difference of the two, leading to specific states of consciousness. For example, a binaural beat of 10 Hz (created from frequencies of 220 Hz and 230 Hz being simultaneously played in different ears) is associated with relaxation and creative thinking.

11.4. Incorporating Natural Sounds

Nature abounds with a plethora of musical experiences: the intricate symphony of a babbling brook, the rhythmic shush of sea waves, or the harmonious melody of a bird's song at dawn.

Bringing natural sounds into your sanctuary can inspire a profound bond with nature. If you live by the sea, leaving windows open to let the sea breeze carry the elegant whisper of waves might be a simple yet powerful way to incorporate natural sound. Similarly, installing a small indoor waterfall or engaging with field recording audios could transcend urban dwelling limitations.

11.5. Exploring Sound-based Activities

Sound-based activities like chanting, humming, playing an instrument, even listening intentionally to the ticking of a clock, can enhance one's engagement with sound.

Sound produced during yoga practices, such as chanting "Om", is known to deliver calmness and enhance concentration. Learning to play a simple instrument like the Kalimba or Handpan can also impart a sense of accomplishment and joy, proving to be therapeutic.

Remember, your sound sanctuary isn't limited to passive listening. Engaging actively with sound can grant you a deeper connection to an incredible universe of resonance and rhythm.

11.6. Keeping a Sound Journal

Keeping a sound journal can be a powerful tool in the journey of creating your sound sanctuary. Jot down your experiences with different sounds, frequencies, heat patterns, or genres over a certain period. Documenting the subtleties in feelings experienced in response to different sounds will give you insight into your auditory persona, and by extension, what kind of sound environment feels most optimal for your well-being.

11.7. Sculpting the Ecosystem of Your Sanctuary

After exploration comes the process of curating the physical space. From choosing a quiet corner of your house to designing the atmosphere with elements like dim lights, comfortable seating, scented candles, or plants, these constituents can amp up the therapeutic ambience of your sanctuary.

Sound equipment is pivotal: a good quality pair of headphones or a speaker system that can reproduce the intricacies of your chosen musical pieces would prove beneficial.

Creating a sanctuary is a creative and personal process, bestowing one with the freedom to experiment and evolve their sound space continually. It's a sanctuary that's shaped not only by a variety of external sounds but also by the internal harmony they invoke. The sounds that worked for yesterday might not work today, allowing for a musical journey of self-discovery and growth.

11.8. Managing Sound Pollution

In the course of creating your sanctuary, striving to reduce unwanted or disturbing noise is essential. Soundproofing your space or using noise-cancelling headphones might be necessary if you're situated in a noisy environment. Choosing a time of day when noise levels are naturally low can also be a beneficial solution.

Foundational to creating your sound sanctuary is the balance between silence and sound, defining, and respecting their boundaries. Silence isn't an absence of sound but a canvas upon which your chosen rhythms and melodies can dance.

As you embark on this symphonic journey of creating your sound sanctuary, remember to be patient. Good things take time, and a personal sound sanctuary is no exception. By enhancing awareness of how sounds interact with your mental and emotional states, you will be one step closer to living a more harmonious, soundful life.